Minnie May and the Jay

Written by Jeanne Willis

Illustrated by Wendy Sinclair

Heinemann

A little girl called Minnie May

M

Minnie
May's
Shop

Was selling jewels from a tray.

tr

5

But as it was a rainy day

d

She ran inside the house to play.

pl

Now on the tray there hopped

a jay

j

11

Who stole a ruby ring away.

aw

13

'Come back!' said May.
'You have to pay.'

p ay

'Okay,' said the jay and he paid **May**.